THERE IS
TOMORROW

D1568812

THERE IS TOMORROW

FINDING HOPE WHEN IT SEEMS THERE IS NONE.

KEITH, ON THE OUTSIDE, LOOKED TO BE A NORMAL TEENAGER, BUT

ON THE INSIDE, THERE LURKED SUCH DARKNESS AND HE ENDED HIS LIFE.

EMMA MARCHESE

Xulon Press
2301 Lucien Way #415
Maitland, FL 32751
407.339.4217
www.xulonpress.com

Paperback ISBN-13: 978-1-66286-772-9

ACKNOWLEDGEMENTS

I am very grateful for God's love, mercy, and grace that has kept me going to be able to publish this book.

To my husband for understanding the time I had to spend on writing and helping me with decisions for publishing.

To my children and their families' support and agreeing to let our story be published.

To my dear friends who have helped to encourage me along the way.

Of course, in memory of Keith. In his sixteen years of life, Keith was fun-loving, handsome, concerned for others, hardly ever had to be corrected as he grew, and so much more. May our story help many who may get caught up in life's circumstances along the way.

CONTENTS

INTRODUCTION

When I was a teen, I remember one time I either wanted to go somewhere or do something. My mom had told me no. I took my hay fever pills, went to the sink with a bunch in my hand, and began getting water. My mom was standing right there and called me out. Now, if I had been serious about committing suicide, wouldn't I have not taken them in front of my mom? As it was, I quit and denied what I was doing, not realizing that years later a child of mine would actually complete suicide.

I will never forget that day as we came home from the hospital the first time back from an appointment since my youngest son, Erikk, had been discharged from being in the hospital twenty-one days diagnosed with T-cell acute lymphoblastic leukemia (T-ALL). We had stopped by the store we had owned back then and my daughter, Tabitha, was still working, meaning Keith had not shown up. When we arrived home, I began getting Erikk's chemotherapy pills ready for him. There were so many, so I asked him to go and get Keith in his bedroom. Erikk came out, but Keith was not with him, so I sent him in again. When Erikk came out the second time, he told me I needed to go in there. He may have said something about Halloween, but I stopped what I was doing and went in.

That is a moment that is a permanently ingrained picture in my mind. Keith lay on his bed, arm ice cold as I touched it, eyes closed with his head turned to the right. His shirt seemed to be tie-dyed, but then I discovered it was a white shirt stained with his blood. I immediately screamed as I ran out of his room. I think if someone saw me from my front window running across the kitchen, they would have referred to me as a mad woman. I think my knees were going up as high as possible to my chest and, again, pretty sure I was screaming.

My husband, Mark, came out and asked what happened. We went in Keith's room together and saw the gun and notes sprayed with his blood on the floor. I hadn't seen them when I had previously been in his room. I called 911 and was able to speak to them, but I couldn't finish telling my mom on the phone and handed it to Mark. I questioned why an ambulance was not sent, just a hearse.

This is a day that changed our family forever. Keith was the type of young man, only sixteen years old, who did not complain, was very helpful, barely got into trouble, and more, but I discovered that he held things inside. I am going to share his notes from when he was fourteen and then when he was sixteen, probably close to the time he took his life. I have been honored to go into schools and churches to share his story as a presentation and it has saved lives. That is also my hope with this book.

CHAPTER 1

———•———•———

A Brief Summary
of Our Story

*There is a tomorrow. Our family's story on the
death of our son, Keith, by suicide.*

Our hope is to reveal the truth behind the lies
our minds try to tell us and to reveal the hope
that lies within all of us.

It's an honor and a blessing to write this
book. It will portray of my memories and a
lot of Keith's notes who at sixteen years old
completed suicide on July 17, 1997. Keith was
my second child who with my oldest, Jennifer,
were from my first marriage. My third child,
Tabitha, and fourth, Erikk, were with my second
husband, Mark, and we are still married

today. My first husband and I divorced when Keith was six months old, so Keith had always known Mark to be his dad. Keith really had no contact with his biological father until he was in high school.

So, we had formed a blended family. We seemed to do a lot when the kids were little. We would go to Florida, Disney World, camping, fairs, grandparents' house, you name it. Keith was especially fond of his grandparents. Keith's first grade was at Napoleon High School. I don't remember the reason but I liked this because I worked part-time in the high school cafeteria and I was able to see him when he ate lunch.

Keith struggled with migraine headaches since he was five years old. He always complained about the noise on the bus. I took him to the doctor for this. It was discovered he needed surgery for something else and we never did discover anything about the migraines. Keith loved school and even made great grades. One year, he and Tabitha got straight A's for the entire year, so we let each of them pick out what they wanted for $100. Tabitha picked a ring and Keith a scientific calculator which Tabitha and I both used while in college (I began college after Keith died).

Keith had been in Boy Scouts and loved it. I remember him ducking down in the car as I took him to his meetings because he didn't want his peers to see him in the short shorts they were required to wear as a uniform. He was very close to receiving the highest badge and spoke of a trip to, I believe, Colorado, but he quit.

Keith played little league baseball once his age allowed and basketball, too, but he quit those, as well, after eighth grade. I remember once in baseball during the last inning with two strikes. Keith was up to bat and struck out. He always took it to heart. In basketball, he felt since he was so tall that he was expected to make baskets, but he was not consistent. I went to every game the last year he played in eighth grade.

Once he entered high school, everything changed. Not only with his physical body as he grew to be six feet two and a half inches tall, but with his outlook on sports and not being good enough. Keith continued football into ninth grade until one day he asked the coach if he could go in. The coach answered, "No. We still have a chance." Keith was so upset. That was the last day he played. I wanted to talk to the coach about it or tell the school, but he asked me not to because it would only make it worse. So, I didn't.

After football, he went to golf, practiced one day, and quit because he said they cheated, and he doesn't cheat. I didn't realize until a few years later that Keith had been bullied in football. He even had our neighbor who had dropped him off for practice go back and pick him up because of being bullied. Keith still had track and the high jump. Keith being 6' 2 1/2" tall, weighed 175 pounds and he jumped 6' 2 1/2". I was so proud to have been there and watched.

Even when we went to the Secretary of State to get his driver's license on his sixteenth birthday in January 1997, we had to make a few trips. I had forgotten his birth certificate and then proof of insurance. In April 1997, he lost a dear friend in a car accident. Some said she was to be his future girlfriend. Looking back as a teenager trying to find his identity, it seemed Keith had a lot of stressful situations in his life during that time.

Erikk was twelve years old when he was diagnosed with T-cell acute lymphoblastic leukemia (also known as T-ALL) on June 19, 1997. We were told by his doctor that he had a 70 percent survival rate because it usually affects two to three year old's, making Erikk high-risk. Erikk was in the hospital a total of twenty-one days, seven of those being in intensive care. I truly believe if he hadn't gone to the hospital when he did he would have died. Erikk only had 10 percent of his kidneys when we got there, was in renal failure, and was put on a Freses machine twice due to the extremely high white blood cell counts.

After his near month-long stay, Erikk finally got to go home on a Friday. The following Thursday was his first visit back to the hospital for treatment. He almost hyperventilated in the waiting room, so they gave him an IV with liquids and let him rest in a bed with no treatment. It was when we got home from this visit that we found Keith.

CHAPTER 2

●————————●

The Innocence of a Child

Keith's notes at fourteen years old

I would like to share Keith's notes now. The first ones were written in 1995 for a class project when he was fourteen years old. Two years before he died.

1-18-95

Do I have any trophies? Yes! I have quite a bit of trophies. I have trophies from as far back as 1984. The old trophies are mostly from bowling. I do have some other trophies, though. I have one from a pinewood derby race, seven from baseball, one from basketball, and four from bowling. I am proud of all my trophies, though.

1-18-95

What do I like to do when it is snowy outside? Well, I usually go sledding or ride a snowmobile. I enjoy the snow sometimes like when it's not too cold. When it's real cold, I just hate it. I don't like the cold a whole lot. I'd rather live in Florida or somewhere where it's not cold often. Well, that is what I do when it is cold outside.

1-18-95

What are my fears? Well, I really don't have any fears. I'm not scared to stay home by myself. I don't worry about dying. If I die, then that just means God thinks it's time for me to get off of this evil place called Earth. So, therefore, I don't have any fears.

1-18-95

What am I going to do on my birthday? Well, I'm going out to eat with my grandma and grandpa. They are coming from out of town to take me out to eat. My birthday is Sunday, January 22. Yes, I'm getting excited. I'll be fourteen. That is pretty much what I will do for my birthday.

1-18-95

What is my earliest memory? Well, my earliest memory would be coming home from school my first day of kindergarten and saying to my mom, "Mom, you lied to me. I didn't learn to read today." I remember being all psyched up and wanting to read all the time, but now, I don't like reading. I'd rather do sports or watch a movie.

2-04-95

What makes me happy? Well, I am happy when I know there is someone there to listen to me. Someone like a good friend. Everyone should be able to have someone to share their secrets with. Everyone should be able to have someone they can act like themselves or they can act stupid around. Pretty much however they want to. So that's what makes me happy.

2-04-95

What makes me sad? I get sad when I see someone who is alone and has no one to talk to about their deepest darkest most personal secrets. I'm lucky enough to have a couple of friends that I can share my secrets with. I hate when people make fun of someone just because they talk different or walk different. And that is what makes me sad.

2-04-95

What makes a friend? Well. I think a friend is someone you can trust, love, help, and will always be there in your time of depression. A friend should care and want to talk about anything that's on your mind. A friend should want to be with you and not be embarrassed to do things with you around other people. A friend should stand by your side at all times.

2-04-95

What am I good at? Well, I guess I am good at cheering people up. I listen to their problems, then give them my advice on what I think they should do. Sometimes I even make them laugh. I try to get their mind off of their problems so that way they can think of only good things.

2-04-95

What is an obsession I have? Well, I love to be outside and play all kinds of sports. My favorites are track, baseball, golf, and football. I think this is a healthy obsession. It doesn't hurt anybody except me when I'm all wore out and out of breath. That is my obsession.

Questions for the Reader's Reflection

What do you think about?

What are your thoughts when you are alone?

When do the negative thoughts start?

Pay attention to the positive thoughts. We all have the choice to choose the positive hopeful path or stay negative.

CHAPTER 3

——•——

Pain From the Heart Mixed with Marijuana

Keith's notes when he was sixteen years old found in his word processor.

As you read these notes, listen for a change compared to the ones when he was fourteen. See if you can relate to any of his feelings, as well.

I am
Courteous. Kind. Obedient.
I like to spend money and have fun.
Courtesy, courage, and music are
important to me.
I get along with just about anyone.
I have a lack of patience, but it doesn't
take much to lift me up.

I like music.
I don't like the freaks.
Money is good.
This is me.
I am.

———•———

May 7, 1997

A scientist might say that a star is a ball of gas which grows with time. They might say that a star is many million light years away. All it does, they might say, is spend its life going through phases until, one day, it becomes a supernova and blows up, then, that is the end. A poet might interpret it in other ways. For example, a star is as high, and only as high, as you want it to be. To grasp a star would be to grasp yourself and look around.

Realize how similar you are to that star. A star grows older and wiser, as does yourself. When the star reaches its prime time, the time when it is largest and smartest, it moves on to the next place. With the departure of that star, all is wiser having known it, and many were touched by its beauty.

———•———

The star is so distant,
Yet so bright.
I wonder if my Sarah is there tonight.

What is she doing?
What has she done?
Why, oh why is she gone?

Did the angel come?
Did she take her away?
But why, oh why couldn't she let her stay?

I bet the angel was so pretty.
I bet Sarah was flightless to follow her.
Sarah was just as pretty, I'm sure.

Now where she is
Only a few know,
But that is where we all will soon go.

Now, my Sarah has wings
And I am sure she can fly,
But the question is, just how high?

She will lift herself up
And fly on down
To watch over this here little town.

Sarah was soon to learn
That the star is so distant,
But to get there, it only took an instant.

●────────●

The future is full of countless surprises, joys, sadness, and miraculous happenings. The past is full of old news that may be useful to some extent. Once something happens, at that moment, it is in the past. With this in mind, don't mourn on old news. The mourning of old news may get you in trouble when the many unleashed secrets of the future catch you off-guard.

Remember: You live for the future; you die for the past.

●────────●

Well, I pulled it off. What do I mean when I say that? Well, I brought up enough courage to ask my parents if I could go to my dad's house this weekend. But the thing that gets me is my mom told me a while ago that if I ever wanted to go, then I didn't have to worry about working. When I told her about how I wanted to go today, the first thing she said was, "What are you going to do about working Friday?" Or it was more like, "But you have to work." Oh well, I think I am going now.

●————————●

It was like any other. The sun was starting to peek through the treetops like it did every morning. For some reason, the sun didn't look normal. Sure, it was big, red, hot, but there was something different about it: it was strange beyond believable. As I sat and gazed at it, I wondered how it would be without the sun. If you think about it, it would probably be quite similar.

I'm sure some genius would make some sort of giant heaters to spread around the planet. Attached to these heaters would be a newly designed light bulb acquired from N.A.S.A. It's jerks like these that make me really mad.

Why not take things like they come? Because those jerks wouldn't make all that money. And have you ever noticed how the only reason you buy things like those heaters is to impress everyone? Once you have one, someone else comes along and buys one to show off to his crowd. That's how it usually goes.

Do you know how it is to live with two parents who fight all the time? Well, it stinks royally! You'd think a person would get used to it after a while, but nope. I think that's why I am so quiet all the time. I know whatever you say, some jerk will turn it around into twenty demented ways, most of them being things that only happen in movies and fairy tales.

I just sit back and watch the stupidity of the people around me. I laugh at them on the inside while I'm completely emotionless on the outside. I've rehearsed showing no emotion for some time now. I've learned to converge all my feelings on the inside; it can save you a lot of pain and anguish. For instance, I have a girlfriend who tried out for cheerleading and made the team. She suddenly got too good for me. It really made me mad, but I just sit back and remain motionless and not say a word. If I tell her how I feel, then I'll become the biggest jerk around. That's what I mean by people turning the truth around.

The sun is burning strong now, but in my heart there is no flame going. I wish the sun would find a fuse and light my heart. I wish I could get rid of this paranoia I have. I don't know why people want to talk about me. That's exactly how society is becoming. It's full of those darn hypocrites. Heck with them. They can all die for all I'm concerned. I've consumed too much of their stuff already.

●————————●

Sometimes, I sit and think about nothing at all. I just let my mind clear out, roll a fat one, strike a bowl, and I am then peaceful. You know, I am strongly against the prohibition of marijuana. It relaxes your body, is not addictive, and helps you in more ways than you may imagine. Read my hemp report for more information on hemp. For now, I must move on and finish doing what I set out to do originally.

I can start writing and just keep punching letters on the keyboard nonstop and I do this so often. I don't think about what I write, I just write anything. That is what is wrong with society today. Everyone is becoming conformed. People don't do anything without first thinking, "What will others think of me?" Heck with them. Be yourself. If they laugh, let them laugh. If they cry, let them cry. If they want to join in, let them join in. But do what you want.

I hate arrogant people. They drive me insane. I am a jerk because of this, but tough crap. A lot of people are oblivious to my beliefs and feelings. I've been called strange, weird, and my mom even told me once that I need to see a shrink. Crap happens.

That is another thing that drives me uncontrollably mad, people are always going to counselors. What the heck is wrong with them, besides the fact that they are ignorant for letting some counselor take their money? I mean, do people actually think that the counselor really cares about them at all? Come on, think about this. Yes, that means put this paper down and think. Counselors go to colleges that "teach" them how to tell people all the same thing. They always have the same solution for your problems. Sit down and talk it out, write your feelings down on paper, or something stupid like that.

Oh well, some day we will die, then there will be peace and matrimony. All will be good. To do good is to be good which means you have to be good to do good and do good to please that lady over in the corner who says you are not good, but you are good, so much good. Ever think what comes after death? There is nothing scarier than not knowing if you are dead or alive.

I've been trying to commit suicide since sixth grade. Every time I try, I awake at night not knowing if I was dead or alive. I don't know what it feels like to be dead, so I don't know what to expect. I have my death planned out now, though. I am going to shoot myself. The first time I tried, I couldn't find a gun. Well, I solved that problem. I am going to make a gun now. I am going to use a mouse trap, drill bit, wood, and my brain. I've got it all planned out.

I hope it kills me instantly, and I know that I am gone. This world is too asperous for me. I can't take it any longer. Family problems, along with all the problems of being a teenager, has brought me down further and further since sixth grade. This way I'll be happy. This is how it was meant to be.

● ———————— ●

Holiday time is here again, and like usual, I have no money. So, I took your idea and made you something. I know it's not much, but it has many uses. For example, you can hang it, wipe your butt with it, blow your nose with it, light it on fire, throw darts at it, flush it, or whatever the heck else you please to do.

Anyhow, I'm glad we're friends. May we continue to be friends, and perhaps someday, maybe our relationship will blossom into something much greater. Who knows. So, may your season be prosperous, and your debtors someday pay you back. Wish your family a happy holidays for me.

Oh, one more thing, always watch your back. I heard there are walking shrooms looking for revenge.

Lots of love,
Keith

●────────────●

What does that mean? Love? What is it? Doesn't anyone know the meaning? For me, it's hard to say that word because I understand the true meaning of it. Integrity. Devious. Yes, that is what it means. People are so openly using the word love. How? I have a hard time telling my own mom that I love her, let alone go around telling people, all people that I love them. So, what does it mean to love?

●────────────●

As the world turns,
The days go past.
Some are slow, some fast.
The hours may get stuck,
But the minutes fly,
And someday, we will die.
The moon is blue

And still, I'm true.
I've got to get on through
To be with you.
If time was stuck,
It'd be just my luck.
I've got to move on through
Cause I'm halfway there.
When a shadow is cast,
You know it will never last.
Lasso your dreams and still be free.
When time's got you down
And you're feeling blue,
Think of me
And your dreams will come true.
If I'm held under
And there's a roar of thunder,
Remember,
I'm halfway there.

•————————•

Since the loss of a dear friend, my heart has been stopped.

My voice is baffled, and my senses disoriented.

I wish for something to do; I wish for it to be not true.

My red heart turned black, my soul quite laxed.

I mourn for something to do; I wish for it to be not true.

The days go by, but still I cry.

If only there to be something to say, someday that I might trade my soul for one that is mended.

My heart weeps for the one who was true, this is why I can't help but to be blue. I wish for something to do; I wish for it to be not true.

As the days slowly evaporate, my heart along with them, the mourning continues, and I am still blue.

I wish for something to do; I wish for it to be not true.

•————————•

As I turn the radio on, songs of my sweetest deceased come bubbling through my ears.

When pictures are all that's left, when you forget her voice, that is when you feel worse.

Even when you feel uncertain, wishing for her guidance, you reach out to feel her smooth, simple touch, but you find yourself grasping air.

Why has this happened? Why can't I change it? Flip a switch or press reverse, if only I could think of a verse.

My tears are all dried out, I simply cannot let it out.

I feel all bottled up, but I am helpless.

In this game, the game some call life, others call hell, we are all victims. This game is unfair, I think they cheat, they grab you when you're on your feet. I thought you were supposed to be down first, not up.

Why is life, life? Why is death, death?
What is life? Why isn't death life or is life death?
Or maybe I am just insane...
When hellos fade to goodbyes,
When laughter shears into cries,
When just a moment recollect to nevermores,
That is when I'll die.

Keith Alan Ellison II

SARAH

Life has a funny way of doing things. I mean, one second you're here, the next gone. How unpredictable it is indeed. But you know, as demented and dumb as it may seem, I think I figured out life. To better help you understand, I guess I'll start at the beginning of this weirdness.

A few years back, I thought that I would die soon. I thought this because I felt that I had a previous life. And in my previous life, I died at a young age. This is a weird thought for someone of only the age of about twelve. As weird as it may seem, I really believed that. I haven't yet begun to figure it out, until now.

Now, I think I finally figured it all out thanks to a dream I had last night. I think I might have died in my sleep, or come close to it. I had a dream about Sarah. I'm sure it was her, although it was really dark and I couldn't see anything. I could, however, feel or sense another presence. This other was scared, confused, and yet wonderful. I then saw a hand come into the light and I right away recognized it to be the hand of Sarah. She was motioning for me to look to my right. After a second or two, I did. At that same instant, I turned my head. I realized I was looking at my alarm clock. It was going off, and the time said 6:30 a.m.

I had a reoccurring line going over and over in my head, "Break on through to the other side," which is a line from a Doors song. At first, I was thinking about the song, then it hit me. How odd just this one line kept going over and over. I realized what the person in the dream, the finger, and the line all meant. Sarah is scared and needs someone to guide her to heaven. I believe that's why she was in that dream. She pointed to distract my attention, and that's when I came back to this world. She's giving me a chance to do something she never got to do, say goodbye. This is where the line comes in. It was her way to ask me if I would help her.

Well, I will. I will break on through to the other side. Although I haven't told anyone what I am doing, I figure someone will discover this and pass it around. If I told people face to face they would call me insane. So, I guess this is goodbye until we meet again. I'm going to walk Sarah to the gates of heaven, so that we shall enter together.

Lots of love and sincerity,
Keith A. Ellison

•————————————•

Life's got me down
So down I carry a frown
When it seems all is gone
Well, it's been fun
It is time to depart
As I leave you my heart
And carry on forever and ever
Please don't mourn
For I did not warn
And if you mourn
You mourn
Now, take this to say goodbye
For now, I must fly
Take my hand as I do stand
And think of how grand it's been
The angels have wings
And I shall sing
Of how much you all meant to me

Please look around
There's not a sound
I think I'm found
Never forget
How it once was....

Written by: Keith Ellison

⚫———————⚫

Time Is Once Again Here
It is time for me to depart.
Please don't mourn,
I have left with you in my heart.
All must go at one time or another.
Some will know when, some will not.
I will.
I leave with peace with all,
But my mind is gone.
I can't think clear
Nor do I want to fear anymore.
Society is corrupt
And all is done.
News is news
And love is love.
But please still love me

After you've heard the news.
When the song is sung
And the pain is vain,
I'll be gone and sane.
You can call after with why's,
But in the end,
Everyone dies.

Love,
Keith Ellison

●————————————●

Grasping the breath from your mouth,
Trying the patience from your conscience.
Eating the foods from your likes and even
your dislikes.
When the moment came and time was gone,
There was a pause.
I can remember the past.
I can forget the future.
What am I thinking?
I am me,
And me am I
Even after I die.
The time is now here.

This pad of paper will soon retire.
Myself, my soul, my mind, will continue on.
Through the gates of heaven, I stride.
My friends and family my only pride.
It is time for me to die.

———•———

Mom,

I will always love you and never forget that! I can't begin to explain why I did this. I can only begin to try. I tried to take my life as early as sixth grade. Life is too tough, and you can say I'm a quitter if you'd like. This is my only way out and I shall seek it.

> Lots of love,
> Your son,
> Keith
> I love you!

CHAPTER 4

———•———•———

Pointing to the Truth Amongst the Lies

Summarizing Keith's Notes

See if you can relate. Notice at fourteen, he believed in counselors, even counseled himself. At sixteen, that all changed.

Compliant Child

Keith hardly complained and was agreeable much of the time too.

An example of this is to melt into the demands of other people. They minimize their differences to not rock the boat.

Keith held everything inside. He seemed to have been tormented by his negative thoughts and if he would have shared them, could he possibly be here today?

Who is your person that you can share anything with?

Blended Family

I did not realize there was a difference. Probably because the children were all mine biologically.

Keith was not raised in a stepfamily atmosphere until almost high school.

Are you in a blended/step family? If so, do you notice any differences?

Low Self-Esteem

Peer pressure, sports, searching for an identity at this age. Is that normal for a teenager?

Bullied. I didn't know until after Keith died that he was bullied. Have you ever been bullied?

Do you ever feel alone even though you are surrounded by family, friends, etc.?

Inconsistency in Parenting

Parents who argue in front of their children. I believe this happens in most families. How about yours? Would a resolution of the problem help?

Keith expressed he needed courage to ask to go to his dad's house. Do you need courage to approach your parents on any subject?

A week before Keith died, he did not want to go to his dad's anymore. Have you ever made a decision like that? Why?

Showed No Emotions

Keith showed no emotions. He hid, buried his true feelings, scared to be truthful. Why? Keith said to keep from pain and anguish. Have you ever felt this way? Just the opposite is true.

We need to share our pain with at least one person. Most times as we share and listen to ourselves, we see where we are wrong. Be careful who you share with that they are not suicidal, too.

Here are some important questions to ask someone you suspect may be suicidal.

What are your friends like?

Have you been contemplating suicide? Has one of your friends or family members?

Has suicide ever crossed your mind? Do you have a plan? Why would you not want to do it?

Anger

Keith put down and complained about society. How do you feel about society? What do you find yourself complaining about?

Instead of complaining, why not focus on how to make a change? How could you make that change?

Denial of Problem

How many of us deny our problems? What are some of the things we hide behind (e.g., food, alcohol, drugs, cutting, busyness, shopping, etc.)? Any other suggestions? Are you denying any problems and hiding behind any of these suggestions?

Drugs/Marijuana

Keith said he used marijuana for peace. But the truth is, when young people use marijuana, there are side effects that can affect and hurt them as they age.

- Under the age of twenty-five, before the brain is fully developed, makes it crucial years for brain development.
- It can lower your ability to think, learn, and remember. This could last a long time or forever.
- Judgments and decisions are affected.
- Affects coordination, vision, and movement of the brain.
- A major effect is low motivation.
- Can lower a person's IQ score.
- Marijuana is twice as potent as it has been in the past.
- Can be addictive and a person may not be able to stop using it even when having negative consequences.
- Double the risk of depression and are three times more likely to have suicidal

thoughts compared to someone who does not use marijuana.

Keith talked about being paranoid. How about you? Have you tried marijuana? After discovering how it can hurt you, will you continue?

Music

Some of the music Keith listened to, including Pink Floyd and The Doors, was very depressing and contained subliminal messages.

What kind of music do you listen to? Is it the words to the songs, the beat, or both that you like? What type would you listen to so it can help you be upbeat?

Loss of Someone Close/Grief

Have you lost someone close (by death, abandonment, etc.)? Your mom? Dad? Brother? Sister? Grandparent? Boyfriend? Girlfriend? Friend? Even a loss of a pet is a form of grief.

Looking back over our lives, I believe Keith suffered from clinical depression. Keith mentioned going to school and seeing an empty chair in the classroom of his friend who had died. His grades began to fall to some E's. Where Keith went to school an E was the lowest grade. Keith had never gotten an E ever.

Confusion

Keith felt a dream he'd had was meant for him to take his life. We can have confusion for a short time while in grief and forgetfulness, too.

What would the reactions of all your family and friends be if they were to lose you?

KEEPING

KEEPING
E
I
T
H

KEEPING

EVERYTHING

I

T

H

KEEPING

EVERYTHING

INSIDE

T

H

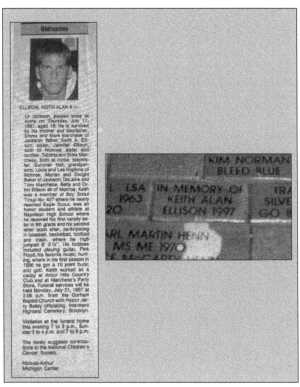

K EEPING

E VERYTHING

I NSIDE

T OTALLY

H

KEEPING

EVERYTHING

INSIDE

TOTALLY

HARMS

CHAPTER 5

———•———

The Impact of Suicide

Description of the pain in our family

Jennifer

Up and down. Stressful and episodes of crying and depression.

Jennifer's letter written on October 4, 2014:

> My brother was obviously hurting when he decided to take his life. Losing someone you love is never "easy." But what he didn't stop to think about is that in trying to end his pain, he was going to cause his family and friends that same loss, pain, and suffering. That he would not get to experience life. He will never

get to fall in love, get married, and have a family of his own.

He will never be able to meet his nephews and niece nor will they ever know who Keith was. They'll get to know stories of him, but he will always be known to them as "the uncle who killed himself."

I ask anyone hurting deeply enough that suicide has ever crossed your mind, **please** look past what you are feeling to those you are closest to, to your families. If you are young, know that you have your whole life ahead of you. Give yourself the time to make your dreams come true.

Ask for help if you are overwhelmed. There is absolutely no shame in that! You are worth it!

Thank you,
Jenna Cunningham

Tabitha

I will never forget when we called her and asked her to get a ride home from our store. When she got home, I have permanently branded in my mind her dad on one side and our friend on the other holding her up. She would walk and fall, walk and fall.

She went to the emergency room in the middle of the night a week or so later for an ulcer. We had her go to a counselor. She listened to the song "How do I Live without you?" By Trisha Yearwood over and over. Tabitha had considered Keith her best friend.

Erikk

Erikk was dealing with his cancer treatments and the havoc they were wreaking on his body. He would get sick a lot, so we made a lot of emergency room trips, and had to go to the University of Michigan, most times five days a week, for treatment.

Erikk had a counselor at the university for his cancer treatments and the suicide loss of his brother. Erikk also mentioned he talked to a good friend at school.

Mark

Mark and I grieved differently. He talked to his friends. We went together to a meeting at the high school on Keith's death and one time to a Survivors of Suicide meeting together.

Me

I became involved in church, Sunday school class, Bible studies, and Survivors of Suicide meetings. I even went to counseling, though it took a few counselors to find the right fit for me. This was such a tough loss on me that the first Christmas I struggled with thoughts of suicide myself. Like Keith's note to me, "Too much pain, life was too tough!" I am so glad that God and other support systems helped me through.

A note by his grave

There was a note left by his grave shortly after Keith died. The writer shared that they were contemplating suicide, but they saw parents, siblings, aunts, uncles, grandparents, cousins, classmates, and friends of the family all grieving, all impacted by this loss, and they couldn't do that to their family or friends.

I would see other classmates at the grave as I went out there, too. Saddened and hurt. All impacted greatly by this loss. Suicide is a very selfish act.

I read this once and have never forgotten it:

"Suicide is a permanent solution to a temporary problem." Unknown

CHAPTER 6

Hope

HAVING

O**NLY**

Positive

E MOTIONS

Hope is to anticipate, to have confident expectations, to have faith.

We are guaranteed hope and a future.

Choose it!

Talk about it; confide in someone positive!

We give out a scholarship every year in memory of Keith. We ask for the students to write an essay about peer pressure. Here are some quotes from a few of them:

> "Peer pressure encourages a person to change his or her attitudes, values, and behavior in order to click with a specific crowd or group."

> "Peer pressure has lost the focus of many students; preventing them from being themselves and from being accepted for who they truly are as an individual."

> "There are always other students around who need a true friend like you."

> "Act like what you do in your life not just improves yourself, but others as well."

"Don't spend your life chasing to be like someone else."

"Don't regret your actions you make because they can follow you the rest of your life."

Questions for the Reader's Reflection

What do you do when you are filled with anxiety, anger, or grief?

How can you stretch yourself from being self-focused?

How can you press beyond any negative feelings?

Our brain is our most powerful organ.

We can choose right thoughts to think.

Sometimes we just need to get our focus back.

We can all get back up. It may be slow, but we can do it!

Who is your person that you could call?

What are some examples of choosing positive thoughts?

CHAPTER 7

•————————•

Survivors of Suicide

Where is our family at today?

Jennifer

Out in the workforce, has four beautiful children, and just newly became a grandma!

Tabitha

Detective sergeant in public safety that includes the fire department. She has two sons. She had been involved with the Big Sister Program, created the Hero Program for children, is active in The Law Enforcement Torch Run for Special Olympics, and does much volunteering to help others in many ways.

Erikk

A survivor of leukemia! Married with three beautiful children. Erikk has a great job, too.

Mark and I

Recently retired and traveling. Enjoying our expanding family with our children, grandchildren, and great-grandchild. We even decided to add to our home with a goldendoodle named Abbie Faith!

I have been sharing this story in a PowerPoint presentation in churches and schools. I have seen many lives changed and saved through the presentations.

CHAPTER 8

———•———

Who Are You?

What are your gifts and talents?

We are all born with individual gifts and talents and some even very unique. We all have a purpose in life. What is yours?

What are you good at without much effort?

What is something you really enjoy doing?

How did you play as a child?

Any certain thing you can remember that you did a lot and really enjoyed?

Maybe it's something you feel at peace doing. You don't struggle much with it because it comes naturally. Or maybe time seems to fly by when you do it.

For me, I used to play school with me as the teacher. I would use a chalkboard or shut the curtains in the living room to watch some boring informative television specials. I did not realize this until my thirties because as a teenager, I was too busy being a teen and then working and raising my children in my twenties. In my thirties, I began leading Bible studies after attending many myself for a few years. I love it and it comes naturally for me, but yes, I have to study, too!

As far as college goes, I suggest if you are not sure what you'd like to be while attending college, just take the basic courses you need for credits. Tabitha went to college to become an entrepreneur. She had wanted to buy our store back or have her own business, but she ended up changing courses to become a police officer.

I want to share a story that Keith wrote for school. I believe after reading Keith's writings, he could have been a writer. Do you see this, too?

This is the story of a man named Pete. Pete lived in the small town of Napoleon. He was born and raised there. One day, Pete decided to take a vacation. He decided to drive all the way to Florida. Since he had never been outside of Napoleon before, this was going to be very exciting. As Pete was soon to discover, exciting wasn't quite the word to explain it. He found that there are many strange and unusual laws which are about as unexplainable as the Bermuda Triangle.

Pete started his trip in Ohio. While driving through Ohio, he came upon Clinton County. Here, he passed a man leaning against the outside wall of a McDonald's fast food restaurant, eating a hamburger. Within seconds, a police car came flying up to the man and came to an abrupt stop. The policeman jumped out of the car and began to read the man his rights. The cop told the man that he was arresting him for violation of the law which states that in Clinton County, it is illegal to lean against a public building.

Pete continued on his trip, driving through Indiana next. While he was driving through the town of Elkhart, he caught a glimpse of a police raid taking place inside of a barber shop. Out of curiosity, Pete decided to stop and see what was going on. The barber was being hauled out in cuffs and chains. The policeman was reading the barber his rights, and mentioned that the barber had threatened to cut off a little boys ears. Elkhart, Indiana has a law which makes threatening to do such a thing illegal.

When Pete came to the town of Owensboro, Kentucky, he noticed a woman being arrested because she had just purchased a new hat without first letting her husband try it on. In the town of Frankfort, Kentucky, a man was being arrested for shooting the tie off of a policeman. Frankfort has a special law which specifically makes this illegal.

After leaving Kentucky, Pete came to Tennessee. While driving through this town, he saw a woman driving a car which was only going about five miles per hour. The ironic thing about this, though, was that there was a man running in front of the car waving red flags and yelling, "Watch out! Woman driver!"

Pete saw a young man standing on the sidewalk and asked him what was going on. The young man told Pete that in order for a woman to drive through Memphis, there had to be a man walking or running in front of the car waving red flags and warning motorists and pedestrians to be alert. While Pete was sitting there talking to the young man, he noticed a car speed by, but the driver was asleep. He was followed by a policeman. The young man explained to Pete that there is a law in Tennessee that makes it illegal to drive a car while asleep.

Pete came to Georgia next. He saw the most bizarre thing in his life here. He saw a man kicked out of church because all he had brought with him was his Bible. This confused Pete. He discovered it is a misdemeanor in Georgia to attend church worship on Sunday without being equipped with a loaded rifle.

When Pete came to Ft. Lauderdale, Florida, he saw a horse tied to a lamppost and a policeman wrote out a ticket and placed it on the saddle. When the owner of the horse came out of the store and saw what was going on, he demanded an explanation. The policeman reminded him that Ft. Lauderdale requires all horses to be equipped with horns and taillights.

Pete had finally reached Florida, and now it was time for him to go back home to Napoleon, Michigan. When he got home, he gave his wife a big kiss. After all, he hadn't seen her for a week. As he was kissing his wife, a Napoleon Township policeman tapped him on the shoulder and handed him a reprimand. Pete demanded to know what he had been reprimanded for, and the policeman reminded him of the law in Michigan which makes it illegal to kiss your wife on Sunday, and this was Sunday.

Pete had taken the trip he had always wanted to take, and learned many new things from it. Of the many things he learned, he will never forget about the many strange and unusual laws which exist in our society.

I hope that by sharing our family's story through mine and Keith's voices that you can see how life can deal us some pretty hard blows. How important our children need the support of all of us during these times. Death among young people has increased as well as death by suicide. We parents and even teachers can get caught up in the busyness of life and not see what is going on around us. Grief can put someone over the edge, especially when we stuff our feelings inside. Sure, some like Keith are very good at hiding their pain, even to those closest to them, but we all need to be available, communicate, and put our priorities in the proper perspective. Our children need unconditional love and consistency in their lives.

About the Author

Emma and her husband, Mark, live in Michigan. They have raised four children, Jennifer, Keith, Tabitha, and Erikk. They are the proud grandparents to nine grandchildren and one great-grandchild. Emma has graduated with an Associate of Arts Degree and had facilitated a Survivors of Suicide support group for six years. Emma has been a public speaker at many events and teaches ladies Bible studies.

Emma has spoken to many different audiences and her compassion is for women, marriages, teens, grief, and more. Emma is motivated by a pure compassion to help hurting people and she loves to encourage and uplift others by revealing how God continually heals her.

If you would like to have Emma come and speak at your school, church, or event, please

contact her by email at <u>emmamspeaks@</u>
<u>yahoo.com</u>.

CPSIA information can be obtained
at www.ICGtesting.com
Printed in the USA
BVHW011749280223
659407BV00014B/194